STARTERS

ANCIENT EGYPT

Written by
Nick Pierce

Illustrated by
Andy Rowland

This edition published MMXVIII by Scribblers,
an imprint of The Salariya Book Company Ltd
25 Marlborough Place,
Brighton BN1 1UB
www.salariya.com

SCRIBO BOOK HOUSE SCRIBBLERS

© The Salariya Book Company Ltd MMXVIII

PB ISBN-13: 978-1-912006-90-8

1 3 5 7 9 8 6 4 2

A CIP catalogue record for this book is available
from the British Library.

Printed and bound in Malaysia.

Printed on paper from sustainable sources.

Visit
www.salariya.com
for our online catalogue and
free fun stuff.

Contents

Introduction

The rich civilisation of ancient Egypt lasted for more than 3,000 years. The ancient Egyptians were skilled builders and metalworkers, and they discovered how to blow glass and make paper. They also worked out how many days make one year – the first calendar! We know so much about them because it is written in hieroglyphs – their picture writing script. Egyptian pharaoh kings led mighty armies but, by 30 BC, the Romans had invaded and defeated Egypt.

Egypt is in the desert lands of north Africa. Its people live along the narrow, fertile banks of the River Nile. The Nile is the longest river in the world, roughly 6,650 kilometres (4,132 miles). In ancient Egypt, the river was used as a highway to transport goods.

Memphis was the first capital city of ancient Egypt. It is where many great pyramids and tombs were built for the pharaohs. Thebes became the capital city later. Opposite Thebes, on the other side of the River Nile, was the Necropolis, or "city of the dead", the site of the royal tombs.

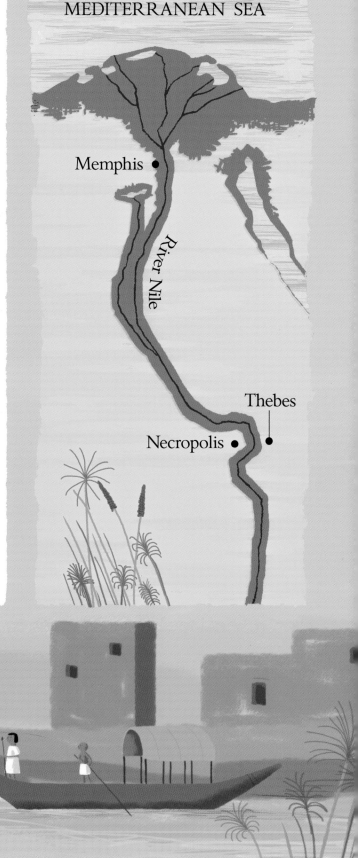

MEDITERRANEAN SEA

Memphis

River Nile

Thebes

Necropolis

On each spread you will have to look for different objects in the main picture.

▲ October
Once the floods drained away, farmers could plough the fields and sow their seeds.

▲ April
By April, the corn was ready to harvest. Farmers cut it with flint-toothed sickles.

Farming

The farming year in ancient Egypt was divided into three seasons: flood time, seed-sprouting time and harvest. At flood time, the farmers' fields were under water so they could not work on their land. During this time, they were expected to work for the pharaoh building new roads, or helping to build his pyramid tomb.

Wheat and barley crops were made into bread and beer.

Tax was paid in gold or grain, or by doing work for the pharaoh.

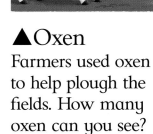

▲Oxen

Farmers used oxen to help plough the fields. How many oxen can you see?

All crops need water. Farmers dug canals into their fields so that water from the River Nile could reach the crops.

▲Pyramids

The ancient Egyptians lived on the east side of the river. The west bank of the river is where the dead were buried. Can you see a pyramid in this picture?

◀Farm workers

The soil was ploughed by oxen, or turned over using digging sticks. Can you see the diggers in this picture?

7

▲Bricks

Bricks were made from Nile mud and chopped straw. They were shaped in moulds and left in the sun to bake dry.

Houses were made of mud bricks. Only temples and tombs were built of stone.

Egyptians were the first people to keep cats as pets. The cat goddess was called Bastet.

Egyptians at Home

A safe, happy family life was very important to ancient Egyptians. Men were craftworkers or farmers. Women worked at home, spinning thread and weaving cloth. Most children were taught skills at home. Boys learned their father's craft or trade. Girls learned housekeeping and childcare skills.

How many cats can you find in this picture?

◀Toys

Can you see the children's wooden toy?

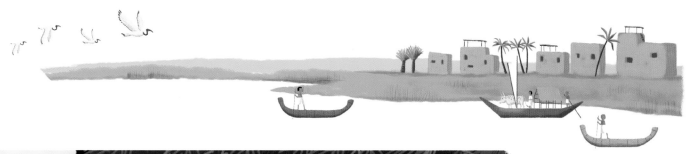

▲The Nile
The Nile was ancient Egypt's great highway. Everything was transported by boats or ships on the river.

▲Food
Food was grown or hunted and fished.

▲Bread
Wheat was ground between two stones to make flour. It was then mixed with water to make into bread dough, then baked in an oven. Can you see a woman making bread?

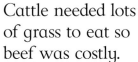

Cattle needed lots of grass to eat so beef was costly.

9

Pyramid

Huge stone pyramids were built as tombs for Egypt's pharaohs or kings. Pyramids had a square base and four sloping sides. The 'Great Pyramid', built for the pharaoh Khufu, has over two million blocks of stone in it. Each huge block weighs about 2 tonnes (2.5 tons).

Can you find...?

▲ Workers

Teams of workers had to drag each huge stone into place. How many workers can you see in this picture?

Scribes

Scribes made lists of each day's work and the tools and materials used by each work gang.

▲ Tunnels

Tunnels inside the pyramids led to the burial chamber of the pharaoh. Fake tunnels were also built to trick tomb-robbers. Can you see the hidden tunnels?

Great Pyramid

About eighty pyramids from ancient Egypt still exist. The largest and best-known is the 'Great Pyramid' at Giza.

Pharaoh

▲Royal court

The pharaoh sat on a raised throne to receive visitors from distant lands. Can you see the pharaoh's visitors bringing gifts?

▲Leisure

Great feasts were held in honour of foreign visitors, or to celebrate weddings, births or religious festivals. Guests ate roast duck, stewed deer, lettuce, onions and honey cake. Musicians, dancers and acrobats entertained them.

▶Musicians

How many of the pharaoh's musicians can you see?

◄ Pharaoh's day

The pharaoh made offerings of food and drink to gods and goddesses in the temples. Can you see offerings of food?

▲ Gifts

Defeated rulers had to send yearly gifts to the pharaoh. Can you see this gift — a giraffe?

A ncient Egypt was ruled by powerful kings, called pharaohs. The Egyptians believed their Pharaoh was a man and a god. As chief priest, the commander of the army, and head of government, Pharaoh ruled all. In truth, he had lots of officials to do these jobs for him.

▲ Clothes

The pharaoh's clothes were made of fine, white linen. The poor wore only rough linen.

Craftworkers

Most craftworkers worked on very big palaces and tombs for the pharaoh. Others worked at home making sandals and pottery or carving wood. Gold-workers, wig-makers, jewellers and glass-blowers made and sold their goods in towns.

Can you find...?

Townspeople
Townspeople worked hard. The children helped by minding the animals. How many children can you see in this picture?

▲Everyday items
Towns and villages had craftspeople who made everyday things. No one made their own pottery – they bought it from a potter. How many pots can you see in this picture?

▼Tools
Craftworkers used simple tools like flint drills, wooden mallets and bronze saws. Their work has survived for almost 5,000 years!

Everlasting Life

▲Organs
The lungs, liver, intestines and stomach are taken out of the body. They are dried out and placed in canopic jars to go in the mummy's tomb. Can you see the canopic jars?

Natron (soda)
The body was packed and covered with natron. It was then left for 40 days to dry out.

▲Bandages
The body was stuffed with sawdust or linen. Then it was oiled and wrapped in resin-soaked linen bandages.

Pets
The Egyptians also mummified their favourite animals, especially pet cats. They buried them in special temple cemeteries.

16

▶Shrouds

The bandaged body is wrapped in a cloth shroud and placed in a mummy-shaped coffin.

▲Outer case

The mummy-shaped coffin is placed inside another strong coffin. It could be made of wood or stone.

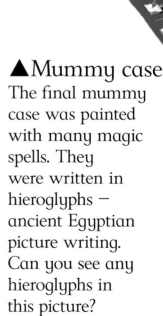

T he ancient Egyptians believed that when a person died they could live on in the 'afterlife'. To do so, the body had to be mummified. It was dried out and wrapped in linen bandages to become a mummy.

▲Mummy case

The final mummy case was painted with many magic spells. They were written in hieroglyphs — ancient Egyptian picture writing. Can you see any hieroglyphs in this picture?

Religion

▲Gods

Many Egyptian gods had the body or head of an animal. Horus, the sky god, was hawk-like. Sakhmet was the lion-headed goddess of battle. The goddess Bastet was a cat. Some gods were only worshipped in small villages. Others, like Amun-Ra, the sun god, were worshipped everywhere.

◄Temples

Temples were built for gods and goddesses. Each temple had a shrine – a special holy statue, where the spirit of the god or goddess lived. Can you see the shrine in this picture?

Priests

Priests and scribes could read and write hieroglyphs — a system of picture writing with over 700 symbols.

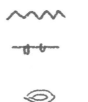

▲ Trainee priests
Boys who wanted to be priests had to study hard at school. They had to learn many temple rituals.

The ancient Egyptians worshipped many gods and goddesses. They built temples to honour them where priests came with offerings of clothes, food and water three times a day. On festival days, statues were carried through the streets. Often statues were covered if it was thought they were too holy for people to see.

▲ Temple paintings
How many images of animal-headed gods can you see in this picture?

Timeline

3500 BC
The first people
settle in the
Nile valley.

2700 BC
Egyptians build
the first stone
pyramid.

3100 BC
Hieroglyphic picture
writing is first developed
and used. Narmer, the first
pharaoh of Egypt, brings
together the Upper and
Lower Kingdoms to make
one country.

2600 BC
The construction
of the pyramids at
Giza takes place.

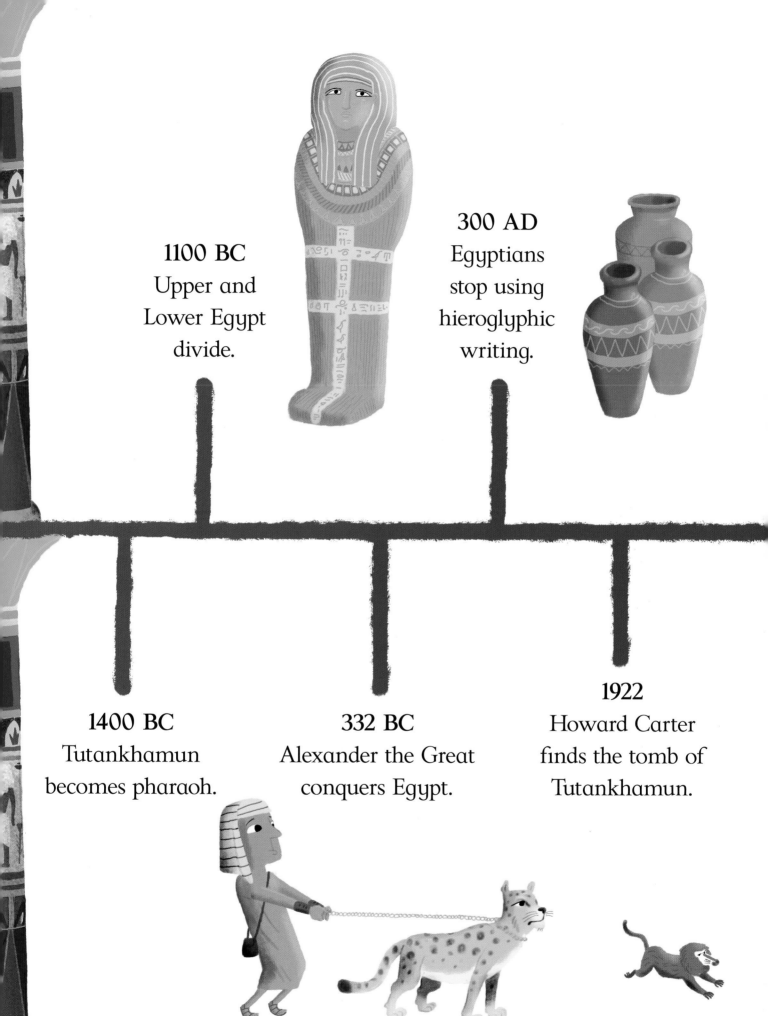

1100 BC
Upper and
Lower Egypt
divide.

300 AD
Egyptians
stop using
hieroglyphic
writing.

1400 BC
Tutankhamun
becomes pharaoh.

332 BC
Alexander the Great
conquers Egypt.

1922
Howard Carter
finds the tomb of
Tutankhamun.

Quiz

1. How many seasons were in an Egyptian farmer's year?

2. On which side of the River Nile did the Egyptians bury their dead?

3. What animal was first kept as a pet by the Egyptians?

4. What were Egyptians' houses made from?

5. What was a pyramid for?

6. Who did the pharaoh meet at his royal court?

7. What were a mummy's organs stored in?

8. What was the name of the picture writing that Egyptian priests and scribes could read and write?

9. What was the name of Egypt's hawk-like sky god?

10. Where is Egypt's largest and best-known pyramid today?

Answers:

10. Giza
9. Horus
8. Hieroglyphs
7. Canopic jars
6. Foreign visitors
5. Burial tombs
4. Mud bricks
3. Cats
2. The west side
1. Three

Glossary

Alexander the Great An ancient Greek king who conquered many countries during his military campaigns, including Syria and Egypt.

Harvest The time of year when crops are cut down and gathered in.

Hieroglyphs Ancient Egyptian writing. At first, picture-signs were used to depict objects. Later, they represented sounds as well.

Howard Carter The British archaeologist who is most famous for discovering Tutankhamun's tomb.

Natron A salt-like substance that absorbs moisture. It is found in the ground.

Plough Turning over and breaking up the soil before seeds are placed in it.

Priest A person with the authority and knowledge to perform the sacred rituals of a religion.

Resin A sticky liquid produced by some trees and plants. It can be used to protect and preserve objects from damage.

Shrine A cupboard-like chest in which the image of a god is kept.

Shroud A cloth that is wrapped around a person's dead body.

Tutankhamun A pharaoh of Egypt who died suddenly at the age of 19. His mummy was found in 1922. His well-preserved tomb, along with his many treasures and belongings, made him the world's most famous pharaoh.

Index